# WHAT DO YOU KNOW ABOUT

# PERSONAL SAFETY

PETE SANDERS and STEVE MYERS

**COPPER BEECH BOOKS**
BROOKFIELD, CONNECTICUT

# Contents

© Aladdin Books Ltd 1995

All rights reserved

Designed and produced by
Aladdin Books Ltd
28 Percy Street
London W1P 0LD

First published in
the United States in 1999 by
Copper Beech Books,
an imprint of
The Millbrook Press
2 Old New Milford Road
Brookfield, Connecticut 06804

Printed in Belgium

Designer       Tessa Barwick
Editor          Sarah Levete
Illustrator     Mike Lacey
Picture research Brooks
                Krikler
                Research

**Library of Congress
Cataloging-in-Publication Data**
Sanders, Pete.
Personal safety / Pete Sanders and
Steve Myers.
p.  cm. — (What do you know
about)
Summary: Explains how readers
can protect themselves by an
awareness of things that might put
their safety at risk, discussing the
nature of safety, threats to safety,
and how to stay safe.
ISBN 0-7613-3265-0 (lib. bdg.)
1. Accidents—Prevention Juvenile
literature.  2. Safety education
Juvenile literature.  [1. Safety.]
I. Myers, Steve.  II. Title.  III. Series:
Sanders, Pete.  What do you know
about.
HV675.5.S25  1999       99-28636
613.6—dc21               CIP

5 4 3 2 1

## HOW TO USE THIS BOOK

The books in this series are intended to help young people to understand more about personal issues that may affect their lives. Each book can be read alone, or together with a parent, caregiver, teacher, or helper, so that there is an opportunity to talk through ideas as they come up. Issues raised in the storyline are explored in the accompanying text, inviting further discussion.

At the end of the book there is a chapter called "What Can We Do?" This section provides practical ideas that will be useful for both young people and adults, as well as a list of the names and addresses of organizations and helplines that offer further information and support.

# —1— Introduction

*Everybody has the right to feel safe. Some of the responsibility for this lies with other people. However, there is a lot we can do for ourselves to make sure that we stay safe.*

In order to protect yourself, you need to be aware of the ways in which your safety might be put at risk. Knowing about possible dangers puts you in a better position to avoid problems. This book explains what being safe means, looks at some of the threats to our security, and discusses what can be done about them. Each chapter introduces a different aspect of the subject, illustrated by a continuing storyline. The characters in the story deal with situations that many young people experience. By the end you will understand more about the importance of personal safety.

# −2− What We Mean by Safety

*At first, we look to our parents or caregivers to protect us. As we grow up, we take on more responsibility for our own safety.*

Safety is one of life's basic needs. To many people, safety simply means the absence of danger. However, personal safety is not only about avoiding or preventing physical risks to your health. It is also concerned with your emotional and social well-being. How you feel about yourself and the world around you is just as important as being in a safe physical environment. As you grow older, you begin to discover what is safe and what is not.

Sometimes we learn through experience. For instance, a small child may touch something hot and find out that it can burn and is painful. He or she will be unlikely to do this again! Often other people tell you about dangers, and you start to understand the risks of a particular situation without having to experience it for yourself.

Every person has a different idea of safety and danger. Some may feel no fear if they look down from a tall building, but others may be terrified. We often think of dangers to our security in an exaggerated way, such as monsters. But in reality, threats to our safety are more ordinary. With common sense many of these can be avoided.

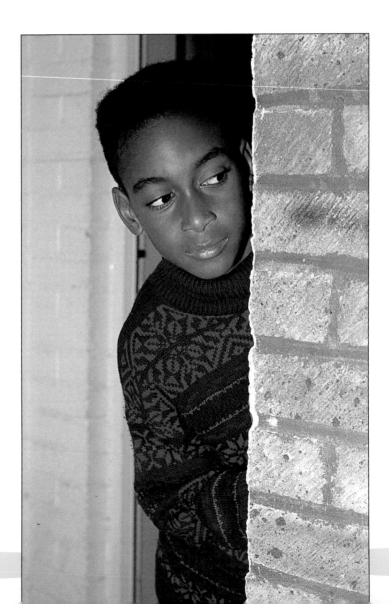

Sometimes imagined danger can be as frightening as real danger.

4

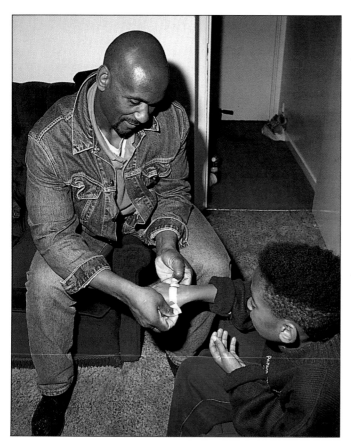

## THE WORD "ACCIDENT" MEANS SOMETHING UNEXPECTED HAPPENING BY CHANCE.

An accident might be the result of taking unnecessary risks or failing to take simple precautions. Or it may be that the person is unaware of the danger, or simply thinks, "It won't happen to me." With a little more caution, Mr. Gardner could have avoided falling off the ladder.

## IMAGINED DANGERS CAN SEEM VERY REAL.

Jayne has scared Max by pretending to be a ghost. Being able to tell the difference between situations where there is an actual risk to your safety and those in which the danger is in your mind is important. Recognizing this can help you avoid possible problems and prevent unnecessary anxiety.

### CASE STUDY:
### CHARLIE, AGE 12

"I used to be terrified of the dark. I'd imagine all sorts of monsters and things hiding in the shadows. I couldn't sleep without a light by my bed. Although people said it was silly, I was still scared. One night, I decided to try to sleep without the light on. I was frightened at first. My eyes could make out shapes in the dark, but I kept telling myself that they were just furniture and toys. It was much easier than I'd thought. After a few nights, I was used to it. It was OK."

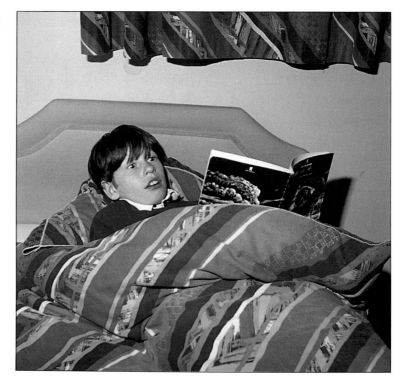

# −3− Safety Around the House

*Did you know that most accidents happen at home? Did you also know that most of them can be avoided?*

Most of us assume that our home is a place where we can feel comfortable and protected. Because it is the one place where we expect to feel safe and secure, we often forget to take precautions that could help prevent accidents at home. It is important not to take home safety for granted. Everybody has a part to play; we all have a responsibility to help each other and ourselves.

Some of the ways in which you can make sure you are safe around the house may seem obvious, but are sometimes easy to forget. For instance, you should never go near electrical equipment with water or other liquids — doing so could be very dangerous. Many pieces of furniture have sharp edges and corners on which you could hurt yourself if you run around inside the house. It is not a good idea to play near mirrors, windows, or glass doors.

Fires in the home can be a particular hazard. They are easily caused by someone accidentally dropping a lighted cigarette or match, or by an accident in the kitchen.

Some homes have been specifically designed with safety in mind for young, elderly, or disabled people. It is worth taking a look around the house and thinking about ways you can help to make sure your home is safe for you, your family, and anyone who visits.

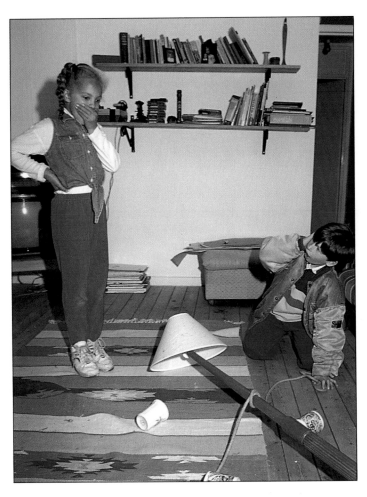

Games can cause damage to furniture, but there is also a risk to the physical safety of young people.

▽ The following weekend, Max went to play at his friend Anton's house.

YOU WON'T CATCH ME!

WOULD YOU TWO SLOW DOWN? YOU'RE GOING TO HURT YOURSELVES.

▽ They ignored Anton's dad and rushed into the kitchen and began to play fight.

ANTON! STOP THAT RIGHT NOW. YOU NEARLY SENT THAT SAUCEPAN FLYING.

SORRY, MRS. MILNE. WE WERE ONLY PLAYING.

I'VE TOLD ANTON A MILLION TIMES – THIS IS A KITCHEN, NOT A PLAYGROUND. IT'S TOO DANGEROUS TO BE PLAYING AROUND.

▽ Instead, the boys went into the garage.

HEY, LOOK AT THIS. COME ANY CLOSER AND I'LL SHOOT.

BE CAREFUL WITH THAT, MAX.

△ Mrs. Milne said they could run around in the yard.

WHAT'S ALL THE SHOUTING ABOUT? WHAT ON EARTH ARE YOU TWO DOING IN HERE?

▷ Max pretended to shoot. He hadn't realized that the drill was plugged in. The drill cut his hand.

MAX HAS CUT HIMSELF, DAD. IT LOOKS DEEP.

▽ Mr. Milne took Max inside and cleaned and dressed the wound. He was very angry with the two boys.

YOU'RE LUCKY IT WAS ONLY A SMALL CUT. IT LOOKED WORSE THAN IT WAS. THOSE THINGS ARE NOT TOYS, YOU KNOW. YOU HAD NO BUSINESS BEING IN THERE.

I'M REALLY SORRY, MR. MILNE. I DIDN'T MEAN ANY HARM.

WELL, TO KEEP YOU BOYS OUT OF TROUBLE, YOU CAN BOTH GO UPSTAIRS AND CLEAN UP ANTON'S ROOM.

### MAX HAS HURT HIMSELF PLAYING WITH THE DRILL.

It is important to remember that not everything is a toy. Many young people have been injured because they have not been aware of the risk, or because they have misused things. You may think your actions are harmless, but you could be putting yourself and other people in danger.

### ANTON AND MAX HAVE BEEN SENT TO CLEAN UP ANTON'S ROOM.

Like them, you may think that cleaning up is boring and unnecessary. But putting things away in their proper place is an effective way of preventing accidents. You may know where everything is, but someone else could easily slip or trip over toys, computer equipment, or video games that have been left on the floor. Avoid leaving electric cords stretched over spaces where people might walk. Items left on the stairs can be particularly dangerous.

**FACT FILE:**
**KITCHEN SAFETY**

- Hot surfaces do not always look hot. Never leave paper or dish towels near the stove. Tie back long hair and roll up loose sleeves if you are cooking.
- Pan handles should always be turned inward on the stove, otherwise they may be knocked over. Make sure they are not over a flame or heat. Electric cords should not be left dangling, as these can be caught accidentally.
- Always use knives and scissors with care. Put them away safely and carefully.
- Bleaches and other cleaning items are often kept in the kitchen. They are very poisonous.

# −4−   *Outdoor Safety*

*"We were playing around in this building site. It was fun at first, but then Jamie cut himself on some metal. We couldn't get out. Nobody could hear us shouting for help."*

Most people are aware of some of the ways in which they can keep themselves safe outside. You have probably been told to be careful on roads or when you are near water. You know not to talk to strangers or to take anything from them. There are many other ways in which you can take responsibility for your safety and well-being when you are outdoors.

Although it can be tempting to play in places like building sites or abandoned houses, they are often full of potential dangers.

Understanding the environment is important. Weather conditions can change very quickly. Remember that protecting yourself from too much sun is as important as wearing proper clothing in bad weather. Wearing the right clothes for the conditions and for the activity you are involved in will help to protect you. At night, for example, bright colors are more visible. Being sensible about where you choose to play, and knowing that dangers may not be immediately obvious, will help you avoid problems. Young people have ignored warnings and have been injured and killed playing on railroads or electric towers. There are many other places where you can enjoy yourself without putting yourself and others at risk.

▽ Toward the end of the school vacation, Max and Jayne went to stay with their cousin, Ryan, and his stepsister, Adele.

▽ They set off for the beach. Jayne hadn't brought her bike, so she rode with Ryan.

WHAT'S THE MATTER? I THOUGHT YOU WERE ENJOYING YOURSELF DOWN HERE.

I AM. I WAS JUST THINKING ABOUT NEXT WEEK, AND HAVING TO GO TO A NEW SCHOOL. MOST OF MY FRIENDS ARE GOING TO A DIFFERENT ONE.

DON'T WORRY. IT WON'T TAKE YOU LONG TO MAKE NEW FRIENDS.

LET'S HAVE A RACE.

OK. BUT GIVE US A HEAD START. THERE ARE TWO OF US.

▽ Everyone swerved. Ryan and Jayne were thrown from their bike and landed on the grass at the side of the road.

LOOK OUT!

ARE YOU OK? DON'T THEY TEACH YOU ROAD SAFETY AT SCHOOL? YOU NEARLY CAUSED A NASTY ACCIDENT.

IT WASN'T ALL OUR FAULT. YOU WERE COMING WAY TOO FAST AROUND THAT CORNER.

△ All three bikes were even as they came around the corner.

▽ The man said that at least nobody was hurt, and he drove away.

I THINK I'LL WALK THE REST OF THE WAY TO THE BEACH.

IT'S STILL A LONG WAY. IF YOU WANT TO SWIM, THERE'S AN OLD WATER-FILLED QUARRY NOT FAR AWAY.

I'LL STAY HERE. THIS IS GREAT.

ARE YOU SURE YOU WON'T COME WITH US?

SHE'LL BE OK. COME ON, LET'S GO.

IT'S NOT SAFE THERE. LET'S GO TO THE BEACH INSTEAD. IT'S MUCH NICER.

△ They spent a couple of hours on the beach. Then Ryan suggested they go exploring.

11

▽ Adele hadn't realized how strong the currents were. She was suddenly too far out, and in trouble.

▽ Adele had to swim to safety. She went to find the others but they were already on their way back to the beach and missed her.

MAYBE SHE JUST DECIDED TO GO HOME.

SHE MUST HAVE. COME ON, LET'S GET BACK. I'M STARVING.

▽ Adele was not at home when they got there. She arrived ten minutes later, very upset.

WHY ON EARTH DID YOU GO OFF LIKE THAT? ANYTHING COULD HAVE HAPPENED. HOW MANY TIMES HAVE I TOLD YOU TO ALWAYS STAY TOGETHER, ESPECIALLY BY THE WATER?

WE THOUGHT SHE'D BE OK.

WELL, I WASN'T. YOU JUST LEFT ME.

▽ Adele's dad offered Adele a burger from the barbecue.

COME ON, EAT SOMETHING. AT LEAST THERE'S NO HARM DONE.

I DON'T WANT ONE OF THOSE. THEY'RE TOO FATTY. I'LL JUST HAVE SOME SALAD. AND YOU SHOULDN'T SMOKE WHEN YOU'RE DOING THAT.

▽ Adele's dad put his cigarette in the ashtray. Suddenly it blew off and landed in some grass.

QUICK, PUT IT OUT! THE GRASS IS REALLY DRY AROUND HERE.

IT'S OK, PANIC OVER. IT'S OUT.

COME ON, I THINK WE SHOULD GET SOME FOOD BEFORE ANYTHING ELSE HAPPENS TODAY!

△ Laughing, they all went over to get some food.

## WATER IS FUN BUT IT CAN ALSO BE HAZARDOUS.

As Adele has discovered, it is important to know the depth of water and to understand how strong currents can be. Water in ponds or canals can be very dirty and may contain objects that could cause injury. Always follow the safety rules in a swimming pool. Learning to swim will help to keep you safe near water.

## PLAYING WITH FIRE OR FIREWORKS IS VERY DANGEROUS.

Fires can cause terrible damage to people and property. Never stand too close to a fire, whether or not there is a flame, and keep sleeves and other clothing away. Material can burn very easily. In some countries, huge areas of land have been destroyed because a match or cigarette was carelessly thrown away.

**FACT FILE:
ROAD SAFETY**

- Always cross the road at a safe point, such as a pedestrian crossing.
- Avoid crossing from between parked cars or other positions where you and the traffic can't see each other.
- Always look around carefully before you cross. Make sure you have correctly judged the distance and speed of traffic.
- If there is no sidewalk, always walk facing oncoming traffic so that you can step to the side of the road quickly.
- Make sure young children walk on the inside of the sidewalk, and that they hold your hand when crossing.
- Always wear a protective helmet when cycling and always follow the rules of the road.
- At night, wear light-colored clothing and/or reflective strips.
- Never play in the road.

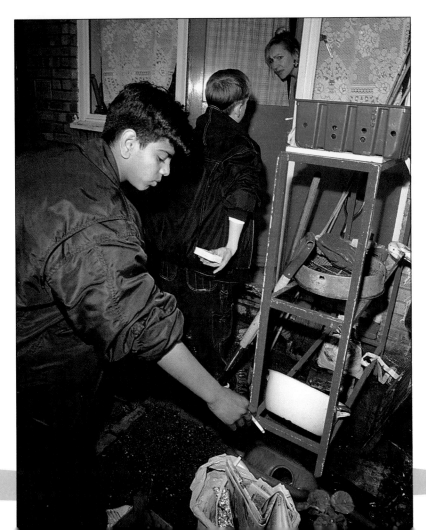

# Emotional Safety

## 5

It is often easier to know how to protect ourselves against dangers to our physical safety than to deal with those that pose a threat to our emotional security. But just as there are practical measures we can take to avoid physical injury, there are also ways of looking after our emotional well-being. Feeling safe emotionally involves learning how to cope with, express, and safeguard your feelings. This means developing your sense of self-worth and respect for other people. It includes making carefully considered choices and decisions that affect your life.

*"Nobody realized what was happening. They all thought I was fine. For ages I was too scared and felt too ashamed to tell anyone that I was being bullied."*

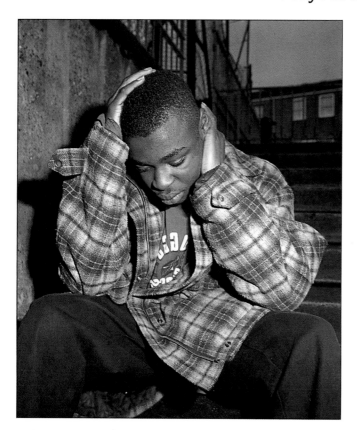

It is important to learn how to stand up for yourself without being aggressive.

Sometimes, people forget how essential their feelings are to their well-being. Expressing them is not always easy. It may be difficult to find the right words to describe a particular emotion or it may be difficult to admit to feeling a certain way. However, support from others enables us to talk about issues and helps us to understand how we feel about ourselves and other people.

Unfortunately, people do not always respect other people's feelings. For instance, bullies may deliberately try to make a person feel bad.

Our sense of security is just as important as the knowledge that we are not in immediate danger. If you know that you are safe at the moment, but think that your safety will soon be in danger, the worry that this might cause can be just as serious as the danger itself.

▽ It was the end of vacation. Jayne was getting ready to go to her new school.

IT WON'T BE THE SAME. WHAT IF NOBODY LIKES ME?

DON'T BE SILLY. OF COURSE THEY WILL. YOU'RE BOUND TO FEEL NERVOUS ON YOUR FIRST DAY, BUT I'M SURE EVERYTHING WILL BE FINE.

▽ Her mom was right. Jayne quickly made lots of new friends. She particularly liked Steph, an older girl.

YOU'RE OK, JAYNE. YOU CAN HANG AROUND WITH US.

YEAH, STEPH'S A GOOD LAUGH.

IT SOUNDS GOOD TO ME.

▽ A few weeks later, Jayne asked her mom if she could have some new sneakers.

I WANT SOME LIKE STEPH'S. SHE SAYS THAT MINE ARE REALLY OLD-FASHIONED.

STEPH'S ALL YOU EVER TALK ABOUT THESE DAYS.

YOU JUST BOUGHT THOSE, JAYNE. I CAN'T AFFORD TO KEEP PAYING FOR NEW ONES, JUST BECAUSE OF WHAT STEPH SAYS.

IT WILL BE, ESPECIALLY IF YOU DON'T MIND BREAKING A FEW RULES.

NO, OF COURSE NOT.

△ Jayne wasn't sure what Steph meant, but she liked her.

ALL THE OTHER GIRLS HAVE THEM. YOU DON'T CARE WHAT THEY THINK, DO YOU? IF YOU LOVED ME, YOU'D BUY THEM FOR ME.

▷ Jayne refused to listen. She stormed upstairs to her room.

JAYNE, THAT'S A TERRIBLE THING TO SAY. IT'S TOTALLY UNFAIR, AND YOU KNOW IT.

WHAT IS THE MATTER WITH HER LATELY? SHE SEEMS LIKE A DIFFERENT PERSON SINCE SHE STARTED HANGING AROUND WITH THIS STEPH.

I KNOW, SHE HARDLY EVER WANTS TO PLAY ANYMORE. SHE'S ALWAYS OUT WITH STEPH AND HER FRIENDS.

△ Mrs. Gardner was unsure what to do.

### MRS. GARDNER IS NOT LETTING HERSELF BE INFLUENCED BY WHAT JAYNE HAS SAID.

People can try to manipulate others to make them behave in a certain way. You may know people who have said they won't be your friend unless you do what they want. Both young people and adults are capable of behaving in this way, and it can create tension and conflict between people.

### RELATIONSHIPS AFFECT HOW WE FEEL ABOUT OURSELVES.

Relationships are important in our lives but making friends is not always easy. Sometimes people pretend to be something they are not in order to be liked. This does not help to build good friendships.

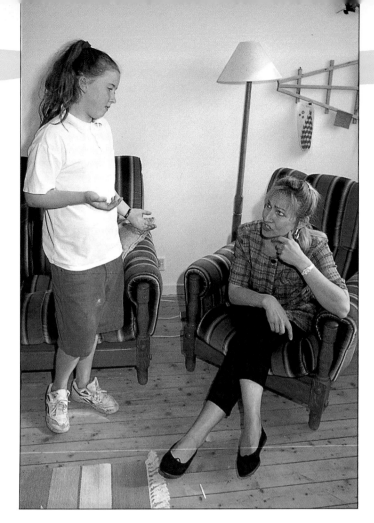

### JAYNE IS CONVINCED THAT SHE IS NOT GOING TO ENJOY HER NEW SCHOOL.

The outlook people have on a situation can affect what happens and how they are treated. People who assume the worst may think they are protecting themselves from disappointment by assuming things will go wrong. However, having a positive attitude can mean enjoying and appreciating situations and people more. Jealousy, or always thinking that what other people have is better than what you have, can make you feel very unhappy. Rather than bottling up your feelings, it helps to discuss them with someone.

# – 6 – Risk-taking and Dares

To take a risk means to do something where there is a chance that the outcome might not be what you want or expect. A dare is a challenge from one person to another. It will usually involve some form of risk-taking. Although there is a sense of adventure and fun in taking risks, it can pose a threat to your safety. Having fun or being adventurous doesn't mean you have to take risks.

People take risks every day. For some they make life more exciting. Not all risks involve physical danger. It might be a case of changing jobs or moving, without being totally sure whether it is the right thing to do. Often people will take what is called a "calculated" risk. This means that they have carefully thought about the possible outcomes and have tried to lessen the chances of anything going wrong. Some people, however, do not think through the consequences of their actions. They act on the spur of the moment or because they are being pressured into doing so.

You do not have to give in to a dare. Doing something dangerous because someone tells you to does not make you a braver or better person. Standing up for yourself and saying no will make other people respect you more. It will also make you feel more confident about yourself.

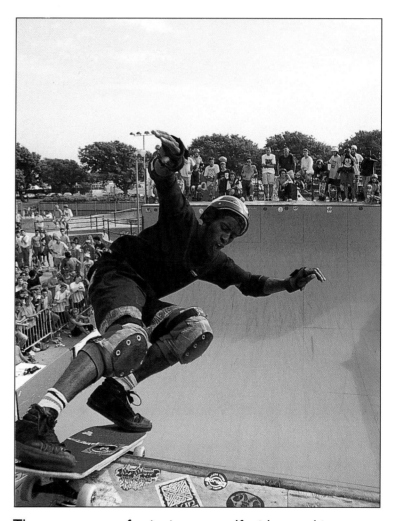

There are ways of enjoying yourself without taking unnecessary risks. For instance, wearing a helmet when skateboarding will help to protect you.

▽ The following Sunday, Max was playing with Anton and another friend, Ben.

I TOOK SOME CIGARETTES FROM DAD'S POCKET. WANT TO TRY ONE?

NO CHANCE. SMOKING'S REALLY BAD FOR YOU.

GO ON. I'M GOING TO HAVE ONE.

▽ Jayne met Steph and the girls in an abandoned warehouse.

WHAT'S GOING ON?

THAT'S LUCY. SHE WANTS TO BE ONE OF US.

I'VE DECIDED SHE SHOULD PASS A TEST FIRST.

▽ Lucy wanted to give up, but didn't dare. She suddenly lost her balance and fell from the girder.

ARE YOU OK?

I THINK SO. MY FOOT HURTS, THOUGH. I THINK I TWISTED MY ANKLE.

I CAN'T BELIEVE YOU MADE HER DO THAT.

▽ Max thought about everything he had learned about smoking from his parents and his teachers.

NO, IT'S NOT WORTH IT. YOU DO WHAT YOU WANT. THEY'RE YOUR LUNGS.

▽ Lucy was going to try to walk from one side of the warehouse to the other on a narrow girder.

STEPH, I DON'T MIND HAVING A FEW LAUGHS, BUT THIS IS REALLY DANGEROUS. SHE COULD BE KILLED.

SHE'LL BE OK. YOU DON'T HAVE TO STAY IF YOU DON'T WANT TO.

COME ON, LUCY. YOU CAN DO IT.

▽ Jayne and Steph began to argue.

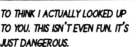

TO THINK I ACTUALLY LOOKED UP TO YOU. THIS ISN'T EVEN FUN. IT'S JUST DANGEROUS.

YOU'LL REGRET SAYING THAT.

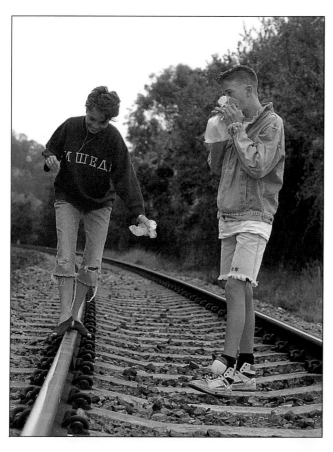

AS LUCY AND JAYNE HAVE DISCOVERED, BEING PART OF A GANG CAN GET OUT OF HAND.

Gang members may dare each other to do things that are dangerous or illegal, or both. You may be afraid of being called a coward if you do not go along with everyone else. But refusing to take part if you think an action is wrong is a brave and responsible choice. Being part of a group can be fun without being dangerous.

SOMETIMES YOU MAY FEEL PRESSURE TO EXPERIMENT WITH SUBSTANCES SUCH AS DRUGS OR ALCOHOL.

These can be dangerous, and both will damage your ability to look after yourself. Although trying some new things can be enjoyable and is part of growing up, you should never feel you have to do anything that might put you at risk.

**CASE STUDY:
ANNIE, AGE 14**

"I used to hang around with a group of friends. They dared me to steal from the local store. I did it because I didn't want to look a fool in front of everybody else, and I wanted them to like me. But I felt so guilty about it. The next time someone dared me, I said no. A few of the others made fun of me at first, but afterward some of them said they felt the same way I did. I felt good that I had stood up for myself."

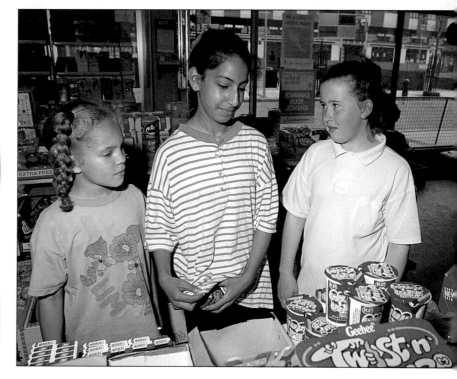

# —7— *Dangers from Other People*

*Although you can take some responsibility for your own well-being, it is important to be aware how the actions of other people can also affect your safety.*

Accidents and other threats to your safety may sometimes be caused by other people's lack of thought or by their neglecting to take action. Most people have no desire to be violent or to hurt other people. Unfortunately, from time to time you will hear of somebody who deliberately sets out to harm others. Some people's behavior can put others in great danger.

People who drive when they have had too much alcohol or taken illegal drugs can cause serious harm to other people.

Some people put others in danger because they are not thinking clearly or considerately. Others do not seem to care how their actions affect other people. For instance, joy riders show no consideration for their own safety or that of others. There are laws and rules to prevent this kind of behavior. Health and safety regulations are enforced in companies and public buildings, such as schools. These help to reduce the number of accidents and cut down on work which is not up to standard. People have caused accidents because they are not qualified, or because they are too tired, to do a task properly.

▽ Over the next few weeks, Steph began to bully Jayne.

WELL IF IT ISN'T LITTLE MISS PERFECT. WHERE DO YOU THINK YOU'RE GOING?

LET ME PASS, PLEASE. I DON'T WANT TO FIGHT.

ARE YOU OK? DON'T WORRY ABOUT STEPH. SHE'LL SOON GET BORED WITH PICKING ON YOU.

THAT'S WHAT I THOUGHT. BUT THIS HAS BEEN GOING ON FOR WEEKS.

△ Jayne had become more and more unhappy as the bullying continued.

▽ Steph stepped aside. As Jayne walked past, Steph put her foot out and tripped her up.

WHOOPS!

YOU SHOULD WATCH OUT. YOU MIGHT HURT YOURSELF.

JUST LEAVE ME ALONE.

▽ One evening, Max was late leaving Anton's house. He thought about taking a short cut.

IT'S LATE FOR YOU TO BE OUT ON YOUR OWN. CAN I GIVE YOU A RIDE SOMEWHERE?

NO THANKS. SORRY, BUT MY PARENTS TOLD ME I SHOULDN'T SPEAK TO STRANGERS.

▽ Max hurried away. He ran all the way home.

I WAS WORRIED ABOUT YOU. I CALLED ANTON'S HOUSE, BUT HE SAID YOU'D LEFT. I WAS JUST ABOUT TO COME LOOKING FOR YOU.

SORRY, DAD. I LOST TRACK OF TIME. IT WAS DARK AND I WAS FRIGHTENED.

▽ Max told his dad about the stranger.

HE SEEMED ALL RIGHT, BUT I REMEMBERED WHAT YOU SAID.

YOU DID THE RIGHT THING. IF YOU'RE LATE IN THE FUTURE, YOU CAN ALWAYS CALL AND YOUR MOM OR I CAN COME TO GET YOU.

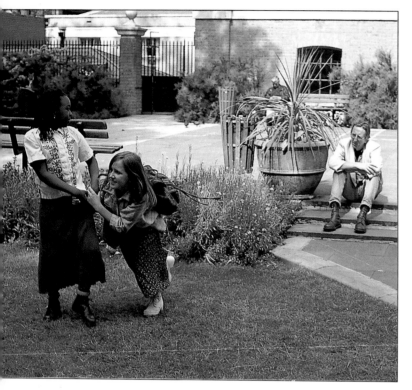

**MAX WAS RIGHT NOT TO ACCEPT THE RIDE.**
Not all strangers are a threat, but it is sensible to be cautious. You should never accept a ride from or go off with a stranger, even if the person claims to know you or your family or if you know him or her only slightly — for example, someone you have talked to in a store or have met at a friend's house.

**EVERYBODY HAS THE RIGHT TO BE SAFE.**
There are people who deliberately harm young people. If you know of someone who is being abused, or if you are being abused yourself, talk to someone you trust about it.

### FACT FILE: BULLYING

- All bullying is wrong.
- Bullying is not the action of a brave person.
- Bullying can take different forms — from threats and name-calling to actual violence.
- Nobody deserves to be bullied.
- Bullying can make people feel very unhappy.
- Most people recognize that bullying is unacceptable. Many schools treat the problem very seriously.
- Bullies rely on people not telling on them.
- Standing up for yourself can sometimes stop bullying. Or, if you are being bullied or see that someone else is being bullied, talk to an adult who can help — perhaps a parent or a teacher.

# Other People and Safety

*"The firefighter said it looks fun, but it's a serious job. They have to take risks, but these are carefully controlled. Safety always comes first."*

We can all take steps to protect ourselves. Other people can and do help us with this. The emergency services — police, fire department, and ambulance — are obvious examples of other people who are concerned with our safety. Very young children and babies, who are not aware of risks, are often dependent on older people to protect them and to teach them about safety.

Other people may need our help to keep them safe. This is why it is important for us all to take safety seriously, not only in what we say, but also in what we do.

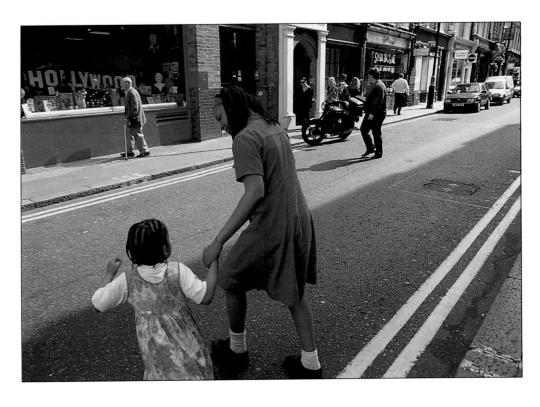

Nearly everything that we buy from stores has been approved for safety. Medicines are tested before they are allowed to be sold or prescribed. Products have instructions for use that are important to read because they have been written to protect you from possible harm as a result of misuse.

If you don't immediately understand a rule, it is worth remembering that it is there for a purpose. However, safety messages do not always agree with each other. For instance, some people believe that violence on TV and in movies encourages young people to take dangerous risks. Others disagree.

▽ A month later, Jayne ran into Steph and her boyfriend.

WELL, LOOK WHO IT IS. WHAT DO YOU THINK YOU'RE LOOKING AT?

WHO'S THIS? IS THIS THE ONE YOU WERE TELLING ME ABOUT?

YES. LOOK AT HER FACE. I THINK SHE'S JEALOUS OF US. SHE KNOWS SHE'LL NEVER HAVE A BOYFRIEND.

WHY DO YOU HAVE TO BE SO HORRIBLE?

SORRY, I DIDN'T KNOW IT WAS YOU.

△ Jayne walked home feeling miserable.

▽ Eventually, Jayne told her mom everything.

IT FEELS GOOD TO TALK IT OVER WITH SOMEONE. YOU SHOULD HAVE SEEN STEPH AND HER BOYFRIEND KISSING.

IT SOUNDS TO ME LIKE STEPH'S TRYING TO GROW UP TOO QUICKLY. SHE MIGHT END UP REGRETTING IT. WOULD YOU LIKE ME TO TALK TO THE SCHOOL ABOUT BULLYING?

▽ Mrs. Gardner could tell something was wrong.

WON'T YOU TELL ME WHAT'S WRONG? YOU'VE BEEN UNHAPPY FOR WEEKS NOW. IS IT STEPH? ARE YOU UPSET ABOUT FIGHTING WITH HER?

YOU DON'T NORMALLY LOOK SO HAPPY ABOUT YOUR DAY AT SCHOOL.

A POLICEMAN CAME INTO CLASS TODAY. WE TALKED ABOUT SAFETY AND THE THINGS WE CAN DO TO LOOK OUT FOR EACH OTHER. IT WAS REALLY INTERESTING.

I REALIZED I KNOW A LOT OF IT ALREADY. SOME OF IT'S JUST COMMON SENSE.

▷ Jayne said she wanted to handle it herself. Max came in from school.

## JAYNE HAS FOUND IT HAS HELPED HER TO TALK TO HER MOM ABOUT STEPH.

Discussing a situation can be a useful way of figuring out a problem. Another person's thoughts can help you to understand your own feelings. This is especially true if you cannot decide whether or not to believe what you have been told, or if you are facing pressure from others to behave in a way that you think might be risky.

## MRS. GARDNER REALIZES THAT STEPH IS RUSHING INTO AN INTIMATE RELATIONSHIP WITH HER BOYFRIEND.

There can be a lot of pressure to have a boy-friend or girlfriend, but there is no rule that says you must. Starting an intimate relationship is not something to be taken lightly. There are issues to be considered that might affect your physical and emotional safety and well-being.

**CASE STUDY: INDIRA, AGE 11**

"It can be confusing sometimes. One person will say one thing about safety and another will say something else. Some of my friends are allowed to do lots of things that my parents would say I'm too young to do. I'm not allowed to watch TV after certain times but at my friend's house I can watch videos. It's often difficult to know what to do for the best. I've been told never to lie or hit somebody, but other times you're told that if someone is threatening you or trying to make you go off with them, then you can make up an excuse or hit them, especially if you're in real danger. I suppose it's a question of thinking it all through, and of deciding what is the best way of coping."

# –9– How to Stay Safe

*"I realized that I couldn't just rely on others to keep me safe. There's a lot I can do, too. It's common sense really — learning to judge situations and avoiding ones which could turn nasty."*

Being aware of dangers to your physical and emotional well-being is the first step toward protecting yourself. At the same time, it is important to keep everything in perspective. Being over-anxious can also lead to problems. Remember also that you have a responsibility toward others. Your actions and decisions can affect their safety as well as your own.

Safety depends both on your attitude and on outside factors. These may include what time it is, where you are, and who else is there.

Many of the ways in which we can keep ourselves safe are very simple — for example, thinking ahead and knowing what to do in case of an emergency. Knowing that situations can change is also important.

Your safety might also rely on taking notice of what people and signs tell you. Although rules and regulations are sometimes difficult to accept and might seem very restrictive, they are usually there for a good reason.

Parents and caregivers may make decisions about the time you have to be home, or perhaps they always want to know exactly where you are going and who you are with. They do this because they care about you, and want to know that you are going to be safe.

Following these rules, and letting people know if you are going to be late, is a responsible way to behave and can save a lot of worry.

# How to Stay Safe

THE ICE IS TOO THIN. IT'LL NEVER HOLD HER.

I KNOW. STEPH, THAT'S NOT SAFE. YOU COULD GO THROUGH THE ICE.

◁ One afternoon, Max, Anton, Jayne, and Lucy went to the park. They bumped into Steph and her friends, playing on the ice.

JAYNE'S RIGHT, STEPH. YOU SHOULD COME OFF THERE.

WHAT DOES SHE KNOW? I'M SICK AND TIRED OF HER GETTING IN MY WAY. SHE NEEDS TO BE TAUGHT A LESSON.

I'M NOT IMPRESSED OR FRIGHTENED. I JUST FIND YOU BORING. I USED TO THINK YOU WERE OK, BUT NOW I'VE SEEN WHAT YOU'RE REALLY LIKE.

IF IT ISN'T LITTLE MISS KNOW-IT-ALL. CAREFUL GIRLS, SHE MIGHT BORE YOU TO DEATH.

◁ Steph started to say something, but Jayne turned around and walked away.

I'VE DONE MY BEST TO STAY OUT OF YOUR WAY. I DON'T PARTICULARLY LIKE YOU, STEPH, BUT I DON'T WANT TO SEE YOU HURT. I'M NOT GOING TO BE UPSET BY YOUR THREATS ANYMORE.

▽ The four friends were going home when someone called out to them.

CAN YOU HELP ME, PLEASE? I THINK I'VE TWISTED MY ANKLE.

MOM AND DAD SAID WE SHOULDN'T TALK TO STRANGERS.

THERE ARE FOUR OF US, MAX. THIS IS DIFFERENT. SHE COULD BE BADLY HURT.

▷ The woman could not stand. Lucy and Max made her as comfortable as they could. Jayne and Anton went to call for an ambulance.

▽ Later that evening, Max and Jayne told their parents about what had happened with Steph and the old lady.

WE WON'T BE LONG. I'LL CALL MOM, TOO, AND LET HER KNOW WHAT'S HAPPENED.

IT SOUNDS LIKE YOU DID A GREAT JOB. AND YOU WERE VERY SENSIBLE TO STAY TOGETHER, ESPECIALLY IN THE DARK.

THE PARAMEDIC SAID SHE'D BE FINE. JUST A SPRAINED ANKLE.

CAN YOU CALL MY DAD, TOO? I PROMISED TO BE HOME BEFORE DARK, BUT I THINK WE SHOULD STAY TOGETHER UNTIL THE AMBULANCE COMES.

I'M GLAD YOU'VE WORKED OUT THE SITUATION WITH STEPH, TOO.

WELL, I'M SURE SHE'LL HAVE SOMETHING TO SAY ON MONDAY. SHE'S NOT WORTH WORRYING ABOUT. I'M REALLY GLAD I STOOD UP TO HER.

Every young person has the right to be protected and to feel physically and emotionally safe and secure.

If you do have any worries about your safety or well-being, talk to an adult who you trust — perhaps a parent, caregiver, or teacher.

### EMERGENCIES:

- Make sure you know emergency telephone numbers: police, fire, and ambulance services; parents' or caregivers' work numbers; neighbors' telephone numbers.
- Make sure you always have change to use a public telephone.
- Learn how to make a collect call in case of emergency.
- Try to remain calm. Explain clearly what the problem is and where help is needed.
- Only make a phone call to the emergency services when essential.

### VISITORS:

- Always use the door chain or peep-hole, if you have one, to check on the visitor before letting him or her in. Never open the door unless you are sure who is there.
- Always ask to see identification if the person says he or she is representing a company or official service, such as the police or gas company.

### BEING ASSERTIVE:

- Being assertive does not mean being aggressive. It means standing up for yourself in a calm and positive way .
- Say clearly how you feel. Try not to make personal comments about other people.
- Keep your voice calm — do not shout.
- Try not to be provoked into name-calling.
- Learn how to read a situation — if it seems to be getting out of hand, walk away.
- Don't be afraid of saying no.
- Don't be afraid of asking for help from others.

## KEEPING HEALTHY AND SAFE:

Keeping fit and eating a balanced diet are important for your health, well-being, and personal safety.

- A balanced diet means making sure that you are eating enough of each kind of food — meat and fish, dairy products, fruits and vegetables, and bread and cereals.
- If you are a vegetarian, you need to make sure that you are still getting the protein and minerals that you would otherwise eat in meat.
- Regular exercise is good for your body and is enjoyable. It can help to prevent some diseases.
- If you are worried about any aspect of your health, talk to someone you trust about your concerns.
- A knowledge of first aid is very useful and can sometimes even save lives.
- There are many courses offered that will teach you what to do — and what not to do — in case of burns, cuts, broken bones, etc.

## WALKING OR TRAVELING:

- Always try to walk in groups. Use well-lit streets at night, even if it makes your walk longer. Never accept a ride from someone you do not know well or trust.
- In trains, sit with other people. Change cars if you feel unsafe at any time.
- If you think you are being followed, cross the road. Stay near other people. Look for someone like a police officer or traffic cop. If you are still worried, knock on a door or try to get someone's attention.
- If you are going to be in a crowded place with other people, have an arranged meeting place in case you become separated.
- Always let parents or caregivers know where you are going and when you expect to be back. If you miss your train or bus, call home — call collect if necessary.
- Make sure you have the correct equipment and clothing for cycling.
- Always wear a seat belt when traveling in a car or, when provided, in a bus.

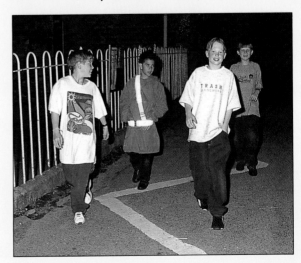

# —10— What Can We Do?

*"At first, I was nervous about standing up for myself, but I think my friends respected me more because I spoke out."*

Having read this book, you know some of the ways in which you can protect yourself and others from risk. Being safe doesn't mean that you can't enjoy yourself. You understand that personal safety also has to do with how you feel about yourself and others. It is important to protect your emotional safety by learning how to express your emotions and understanding how to deal with certain situations.

Building your confidence and learning how to be assertive can help with this. Sometimes people will try to make you join in activities that are not safe. Remember that taking foolish risks, particularly in response to a dare or because you want to show off, can have very serious consequences. You may want to think about how you have handled situations in the past, and consider the things you can do or say in the future to make sure you stay safe.

Adults can also help by taking practical safety measures, such as getting smoke alarms and door chains. They can also be available for young people to talk to if they have any particular concerns about their physical or emotional safety.

Feeling secure and being safe allows you to enjoy yourself to the fullest.

Adults and children who have read this book together may like to discuss their feelings about the issues involved. Anybody who would like to talk to someone else about any aspect of personal safety might want to contact one of the organizations listed below. They should be able to offer practical advice as well as support and information.

### CENTER FOR INJURY PREVENTION

5009 Coye Drive

Stevens Point, WI 54481-5078

(800) 344-7580

http://www.bucklebear.com

### CHILDREN'S SAFETY NETWORK

55 Chapel Street

Newton, MA 02458-1060

(617) 969-7101 x2207

http://www.edc.org/HDD/csn

### NATIONAL SAFE KIDS CAMPAIGN

1301 Pennsylvania Avenue

Suite 1000

Washington, DC 20004-1707

(202) 662-0600

http://www.safekids.org

### CANADA SAFETY COUNCIL

1020 Thomas Spratt Place

Ottowa, Ontario

Canada K1G 5L5

(613) 739-1535

http://www.safety-council.org

### AMERICAN RED CROSS

1621 North Kent Street

Arlington, VA 22209

(703) 248-4222

http://www.redcross.org

### COALITION FOR CHILDREN

Safe Child Program

PO Box 6304

Denver, CO 80206

(303) 320-6321

http://www.safechild.org

# Index

## Photo credits

All the pictures in this book are by Roger Vlitos except: pages 17, Eye Ubiquitous; page 26, Frank Spooner Pictures. The publishers wish to acknowledge that all the people photographed in this book are models.